Smiling at the Executioner

Smiling at the Executioner

Poems by

M. B. McLatchey

© 2023 M. B. McLatchey. All rights reserved.
This material may not be reproduced in any form, published,
reprinted, recorded, performed, broadcast,
rewritten or redistributed without
the explicit permission of M. B. McLatchey.
All such actions are strictly prohibited by law.

Cover design by Shay Culligan
Cover image: Marcus Aurelius, fragment of a bronze portrait,
Louvre Museum, Paris, France, © Marie-Lan Nguyen /
Wikimedia Commons, used with permission
Dedication page: Ἔνδον σκάπτε, "Look within." from
Marcus Aurelius, *Meditations VII, 59*

ISBN: 978-1-63980-454-2

Kelsay Books
502 South 1040 East, A-119
American Fork, Utah 84003
Kelsaybooks.com

For Michael and Geoffrey
Ἔνδον σκάπτε

with special thanks to my fellow writers and colleagues
at Embry-Riddle Aeronautical University who
have so generously supported my craft,
especially Donna Barbie

Also by the Author

Poetry
Advantages of Believing
The Lame God

Prose
Beginner's Mind

Textbooks
Great Works of Ancient Greece
Primary Sources: Ancient Greece, the Roman Empire, Middle Ages

Acknowledgments

Heartfelt gratitude to the editors of the following journals where these poems first appeared, sometimes in slightly different form:

The American Poetry Journal: "A Kenning"
The Aurorean: "Portable Labyrinth"
The Banyan Review: "A Drink of Water," "Synonym for Marriage"
The Briar Cliff Review: "Ocracoke"
Cider Press Review: "Invocation," "Arcadia"
The Comstock Review: "Odalisque"
Drunken Boat: "The Breakfast Piece"
Ekphrasis: "Wash Day"
The Florida Review: "Command Z"
Folio: "Ode for an Ode on a Grecian Urn"
Harpur Palate: "Anthem," "On Folding a Fitted Sheet"
Iris Literary Journal: "On Forgetting Ash Wednesday"
The National Poetry Review: "Cues"
Naugatuck River Review: "The Bath," "Sugaring," "Learning the Scriptures"
The New Formalist: "House on Fire"
Pensive: A Global Journal: "Afterlives"
Quadrant: "Before the Common Era"
The Raintown Review: "Aftercare"
Relief: "Calendar Plans"
Ruminate Magazine: "Empirical God"
Saw Palm: Florida Literature and Art: "We Leave the Beaches for the Tourists, Mostly"
Sequestrum: "The Shadow Maker," "War in Eurasia"
Shenandoah: "Days Inn"
Sky Island Journal: "Smiling at the Executioner"
Southern Poetry Review: "Inventory"
SWWIM: "Where Winter Spends the Summer," "Bad Apology," "The Wisdom of the Cave"
Tampa Review: "Balcony House"
Tar River Poetry: "Parousia"

Contents

I

Smiling at the Executioner	17
Ode for an Ode on a Grecian Urn	18
The Wisdom of the Cave	19
Before the Common Era	20
Ocracoke	21
Command Z	23

II

Aftercare	27
Odalisque	28
Empirical God	29
The Shadow Maker	31
Afterlives	32
Days Inn	33
On Folding a Fitted Sheet	35
War in Eurasia	36
Wash Day	37
Parousia	39

III

Pasty Pool	43
Morning Light	44
Mind Reader	45
Turn Me	46
Layers	47
My Face	48
Leave the Day	49

IV

The Breakfast Piece	53
A Drink of Water	54
Synonym for Marriage	55
On Forgetting Ash Wednesday	56
Balcony House	57
A Kenning	59

V

Invocation	63
Calendar Plans	65
Illuminator	66
The Bath	68
Sugaring	69

VI

Mandatum	73
Learning the Scriptures	74
Cues	76
We Leave the Beaches for the Tourists, Mostly	77
Saudade	78
Labyrinth Walkers	80
Song of Menalcas	81

VII

Inventory	85
Where Winter Spends the Summer	86
Sentinels	87
Portable Labyrinth	88
Almanac	90
Bad Apology	91
House on Fire	92
Arcadia	93
Interlude in Anglo-Saxon Lines	94
Anthem	95

I

Reject your sense of injury and the injury itself disappears.
—Marcus Aurelius

Smiling at the Executioner

As if the open barrel were a lotus;
its roots anchored in mud.

How undeterred
by murky water, it submerges

and reblooms: petals like crystal
glazed and without residue.

As if you never felt something move:
no welcome and prescient ache,

no sudden flexing, no cycle taking shape.
No memory. No calendar. No yield—

because you are the bullet's shield. As if
you have nothing to lose. As if all that you have

learned to love: the beating heart; the mythic glove
of a palm blooming in the womb; the scent that follows

touch—is suddenly dust. Just the open-grinned,
white-toothed stare down this time;

the stayed and steady practice on your knees
of mastering someone else's pleas.

Ode for an Ode on a Grecian Urn

Ode,
let your sorrows go.
Let brides be ravished, trees forsake
their leaves, let lovers kiss and fade, daughters age. Let loss
be the elixir that induces a new legend, new urn-dream:
Forests that seed, mature, starve, and reseed
without our overtures. Let wanting, waiting,
pacing be the rings in carbon dating. A new
museum piece. Imagine yearning bigger than an
urn, bigger than god; desire out of bounds, desire
crowned. Paint it fulfilled, the turning back of hounds.
What good is song if not the end of one man's wish,
what-ifs? I died at twenty-five. So many do. Urn, make
your story new: Beauty is truth when sung to a priest's
staccato voice and tone near a young marine's
too heavy, too mature, burial stone; when love
betrayed makes lovers stutter phrases—sweet
clichés—that they used to say alone. Put it
in stone: Beauty is truth when sung to
the beat of a child's quiet feet
leaving home; when
aging lovers sing
to one another:
Remember when we
used to rock in one another's arms
and we knew god and the devil's charms?

The Wisdom of the Cave

*If you're always under the pressure of real identity,
I think that is somewhat of a burden.*
—Mark Zuckerberg

In the cave, our histories are shadows
on a wall; our memories rote lessons
that flicker and mutate. Fall and spring,

then and now, captured and interchanged.
Friezes like post cards sculpted to ornament
the grotto, endure, resist decay.

When the shadows dance, we point, open
our mouths, as if for a split second, something
shifts, recalibrates. A glimpse of fire and lathe

and shadow makers. Forms beyond hope.
Ideas like sirens singing. Cracks in a wall
that luminate, hint at another source: rivers,

flora and bursts of color, starlings with iridescent
wings, shrubs whose roots finger through mud
for something to drink. A world too fluid to dangle

from rod and string. How could we want its ranges, moon,
its chorus marking dawn, its feathered swirl confusing
predators, its messenger's glad song? Why should we

mind the tether anchoring us; the flame that fixes seasons,
stages night and day, that orients us frontward, ever
frontward, and keeps the constellations in their place?

Before the Common Era

Before Epictetus, the Aztecs, Machiavelli;
before Berkeley, Spinoza, Calvin,
Hegel and Heidegger; before the Bavarian
Illuminati; before Marie Antionette; before Schelling

before Hayek, Derrida, and Bukowski; before the laws
of timeless nature; Kerouac. Before Nirvana analysis
and conceptual tunneling; before subtle physics;
before alternative systems; before god,

I remember we planted some seeds in a narrow
back lot, a trellis with open ties for the sprouts like bait
and lure in sod tiles. And we waited for spring, we waited
for our first child: a new world of water and marrow.

We knelt by terraces, brushing the earth. The air's soft tongue
kept us at our tasks, not missing things unsaid, anthems unsung.

Ocracoke

for J

In a letter to his wife, sure and seasoned,
he said, I will be back. I will cross channels

and oceans and islands and rushing rivers.
And for the rest of her years, his flannel

shirt that she made her own, caught her
tears as they might in a lover's hold.

What are our days, she wrote,
or distances, or promises, or years,

if not one heartbeat measured out
in a country's checkered grid, weave

in a cloth—newly endeared? As once
in Ocracoke, barrier island, barrier

to all that does not hold against cruel winds
and so, not love, which holds and takes

its fortitude from dune-crushing gales. The hush
that follows cruel words; the kiss that cools

like a shore bird in low waters; gestures
of a land without clear borders. A dress

that I saw in a shop and I longed
as we ferried away, as a small girl longs,

for sea winds catching its hem in a gust
of sea spray above my knees. And you wanted

to please me because—I would come to see—
that is what lovers do. Let's go back, you said.

And I noticed the difference in miles for me
and you: what for me was a change in our plans

and a girlish yearning, was for you love's open hand—
a summer dress on a wooden hanger—ocean and sand

that we might reclaim like a sparrow's song
played and replayed. No distances, no time—

I learned that day—no ferry we cannot take
from lover's gift to lover's ache.

Command Z

A shortcut to *undo;* and so the hateful words we say,
hateful because we have not loved someone
so much before—can be reversed, undone, erased.
A dream come true: No evidence. No blowgun

residue. No shadowy pin-print in the chest, where
the pointed tip pierced through. No plaintive call
to cauterize the wound. No sky gods cheering
for a second act. Nature reversed: No crawling

back, no silken trail, no bouquets of fattened leaves
in new host trees with larval tents; branches where we will
leave our scent and later, feed. Limbs in silk sleeves
like spring in a dying season, as if to ornament the kill.

As if, behind the screen, like lotuses, merciless words
did not fix their roots in swampy waters, undisturbed.

II

*Think of yourself as dead. You have lived your life.
Now take what's left and live it properly.*
—Marcus Aurelius

Aftercare

for my husband

For the send-off, a haversack of mounting days:
socks with slip-proof stops, a comb, an unused shaving
set. Hospital kitsch. A folder with paper-clipped scripts

in Livy's Latin: a history of pour turned into measured
drips. Labels like vague instructions or memories
of how and what we were, how to retrieve

our former selves—or not. There is no aftercare
kit for this. Only the fossil imprint: decades
of love's rich lava laying down sediment in its

own hard strata. Winter's cover melted. Proof
of the distress of a cavernous shift—valleys
widened, rivers uplifted. *Aftercare* will bear

the gods' culled crops, a summoning to a seasonal
bell. No longer winter wheat, sweet corn rotations:
Arcadia from grafted stems and dark, inconstant cells.

Odalisque

Early light, the chill of souls leaving. You draw up the sheet
to cover us; the soft of musk, the body's heat
from an air pocket, nudged and wayward. The scent
of fading bleach. I give you the curl of my back, a nonevent.

Yet, all of it art. Ingres and Ingres' odalisque

who drapes a velvet curtain's jeweled sash
across her calf; whose hips turn in a wash
of Turkish hues. A French settee
or this bed: staging we need

to fuel our natural lives. To feel the body lift

to the extension of a kiss. The temporal shift
in calling souls home—stomach, thighs—like this.
Alms, forgiveness. A quickening in canvas or stone:
my open mouth and your inarticulate moan.

Empirical God

God has many names.
    —Aristotle

Start with the known,
the way a child begins.

A child begins by calling
all men *father*. Then, later on

distinguishes. *Father:* burrower,
planter of unharvestable spring.

Mother, first rope
and ring tossed to a budding

glove—a sustenance, like air
or love. Love, that triggering

nerve that in the Greek origin
myth substitutes touch for a god's

imperative: union of sky and sea,
sea and earth. Luminous bodies

coupling like first birds.
Call it *one god, one heaven*

when learned
through its carcass and seed.

Palm. Milk. Soul. Wing.
Palm, fallow field surrendering

its feed. Milk, an ancient
man's mother's plan.

Soul, a rusted bell ringing,
striped buoy bobbing,

bobbing. Wing, a triumph
and sudden cold.

The Shadow Maker

Our goal is to make it so there's as little friction as possible to having a social experience.
—Mark Zuckerberg

is one of the richest men in the world;
a harvester of pearls: our small talk
like algae-rich waters and tides—new births,
divorces, prizes our children acquire—
feeding and keeping the oysters alive.

is a master of illusion: figures in captioned
poses, screen and light; shadows that dance
on cave walls. Dramas that make us muse, lean
in, post notes like medieval glosses in the margins
of someone else's domestic scenes; illuminators
to an epic chant, a rhapsody's god-dream.

is the Ideal Prince, accepting the burden
of princedoms, glory, survival, to jettison distinctions:
good and depraved; monarch and something human
saved. Better to be loved and feared rather than
admired, or worse, revered. A lord who understands
the desire to acquire. A magician with two hands.

is a Philosopher King, able to discourse on goodness,
justice, corrupting pride; hold court on high ideas:
opinion, false truths, reality—a theory of forms
that casts our lives in cycles, fruit and fallow; sinners
redeemed. A god's will altered; a cave master's dream.

Afterlives

Only faces in little boxes now; blinking and peering
into a starless space, not knowing what to do

except perhaps, wave. Our host asks each box:
What's new with you? We talk, in turns.

We share the *virtual* part—meaning
the *essence*. It's lovely. How this half-body

huddle forces us to talk; how we conform,
like grafted stalks, to a new light source.

Dante insists our afterlives will be the *now eternal*.
I study my husband's framed face unselfconsciously.

No one can see me gazing at our years.
My sons, I see, have become men whose eyes

are equable and clear. Time lapses freeze, in pixel images,
expressions like true selves they made as toddlers.

On TV, the Pope delivers the Mass to empty seats.
How alone he looks—in spite of the live stream.

No pilgrims, no Vatican City festooned with flowers;
only police to hold the barricades. And yet, the numbers say,

more watched and listened to the liturgy than ever
attended. On sofas that sag, on laptops, in drive-thru

caravans for bread and wine. An insistence on right seasons if only
to prove we are different from our dogs. We hear a whistle too.

Days Inn

Everything about it says *Economy:*
The rattan headboard; the fibrous spread
catching us in its threads. The walls: thousands
of sherbet-green fronds set against fading
mountain ranges like sketches
from the notebook of a British colonel
drawn and redrawn absent mindedly
then posted all around as friendly notice
of distant, unattainable exotica.

On the television, and perhaps part
of the package: Tarzan and His Mate, 1934.
The treasure hunters have, at last, dispersed.
O'Sullivan and Weissmuller slip—
searing and nude—into a jungle pool. So verdant
and so bestial a scene that Jane's a body double.
Sweet paganism, one critic called it
to thrust a man and woman into love like this
naïve in one another's world until they kiss.

Hardly the English Lord fluent in languages
this Tarzan smothers upturned panting lips
with a desire that covers her like moss.
Part ape, Robinson Crusoe, sometimes Moses.
His role, in any case, is to save Jane
from herself. To teach her how to sail
from vine to vine as though standing still.
And when it comes to leaving, not to pale
from choosing human nature over longing.

God knows this kind of choice sees casualties.
In Kansas City, in a single day, fifteen children fell

from trees while practicing the victory cry
of the great ape. In cinematic style, medics healed
the noble savages with splints. And young boys cried
from their sick beds, all hours, jungle-piercing calls.
Noblesse oblige. Cities, of course, have burned
to choruses like this. *Love* wants a jungle shower.

On Folding a Fitted Sheet

The art, it seems, is in the ease
of mirroring what is measured:

at once attending to, surrendering
to a set of numbers, a fixed but—

when you release too tight a grip—
supple and scented plane.

Tuck the puckered edges back.
Give it a *thwack*. Let it balloon—

a goddess-smelted bloom
of what remains after ablution:

smoke-colored shadows, the stir
of a post-coital myrrh.

Hold as one holds
a picture you would hang

or, as in Prokofiev's ballet: arms
bent and raised, palms open-faced.

Fold it until the edges meet—
repeat, repeat. Walk it upstairs

with the reverence you'd have
for carrying your country's flag.

War in Eurasia

*We shall squeeze you empty, and then we shall
fill you with ourselves.*
 —George Orwell, *1984*

We sleep like guard dogs, one eye open, groomed to unlock
from one another's folds. Older, a cooler grey than our adult
years. My breast, like a forbidden prayer or scent or thought,
presses against your arm. The war in Eurasia rages on. The dull

flicker of the TV; the news anchor's lips tattooed a deep
party red mouthing vowels: A and E, and O—not I or U.
Everything in black and white, or streams of sepia.
We hardly remember the difference between *the news*

and truer truths; the sum of two plus two. Harvest seasons
pass. Dictionaries yield a sulphury marsh gas. Winters sprout
days of halcyon, golden wheat. We yearn for myths that lean on
goddesses of crops, a mother's loss and rage, a revenge drought.

Love is the warrior's call. We knew it in the womb, first breath,
when we were made to choose: a dying art, or this waking death.

Wash Day

after Grandma Moses

So hard to know the subject: a meadow, dead center
of oils in green? Or left of it, this hyperactive wash scene:
milky-white shirts scattered on the yard's mossy edge.
Rows of blanched sheets fluttering from taut lines
that hem them in, that keep the women with their laundry
always receding. And opposite the sheets, a picket fence
that seems to frame the spongy grades of green and lime
and ask us to reflect on—what? Something the women

and the others have quietly agreed to turn away from.
Look how they crowd their way into the margins. Here,
a harvest story: flecks of red gathered into baskets. Words said
between harvesters. Words so compelling that one of them stands
upright to view the other. Is he facing the painting's question?
Or does he only seem to look at him because they share
this tiny patch of goldenrod and green and picket fences?
Easy to grant: this kind of ground that parcels out our senses.

And far, far off from center, a first or last encounter:
a woman stops as she exits a dark, cool shed—
stops, not to adjust to the day's stark light
but to feel the gaze of a man more painted
than she, to feel the thrust of sepia:
his suit, dabbed on like that line of aging wood
outside the shed; like the sepia dresses of the women
nearby; like the silo, sepia and Indian red, that hedge her in.

Roads leading in, but not to the center of life.
Only the large white house, the same starched white
as the sheets the women hang. Windows with shades
half-drawn so evenly that they have clearly been painted on.
A front door shut so tight that it disappears, at times,

as white will against white. The chimney
(and so, the hearth) an afterthought
in browns and burgundy. Is this the cache of colors then

that comes with knowing one's lot? The end of looking
east or west? The fertile ground fenced off?

Parousia

A presence and this morning's shower
lingering like mist before my eyes.

As if to flaunt my unpreparedness—towel
for a turban; my face, a pale and open sky—

I greet them at my door. *Picture the scene,*
they chant, *a harlot sitting on the back*

of a fearsome beast. A terrible waking-dream
of a naked whore of false beliefs straddling

the back of a wild boar: metaphors for the Parousia.
Standing on my porch, I wonder if they are attached,

newlyweds perhaps, who fell in love over scripture
or perhaps they present themselves like this: A Final Act

to test my interest in the text, or in the man. Sun-bleached
hair, finger-combed, his face unexpectedly tanned,

the curl of his lip. *Witness,* he purrs. *Jehovah.* I accept
his *Two Destinies* pamphlet; offer them water.

As for ancient debts, healing, forgiving, I am
going—have already gone—toward the living.

III

Don't stumble over something behind you.
　　　　—Seneca

Pasty Pool

I lie in my own pasty pool
like a lamb in a druid's bed.
Layer by layer, thread
after thread, I shed
and shed. O, press me
between your palms again!
Deliverer, be delivered.
Without your need, without
a blight to beautify,
what am I?

Answer to riddle in reverse: **paos fo rab**

Morning Light

In this morning
light, I am almost
transparent, a sheet
of shimmering
snow that dries
your tears—once
in your tight embrace,
twice in your lingering
scent, this care, this
newfound air.

Answer to riddle in reverse: eussit

Mind Reader

Mind reader, tell me
what I am thinking.
Open yourself
to my slow descent,
my inky lips,
my endless sinking
down
your broad white breast
your woven twine
your cleaving spine.

Answer to riddle in reverse: yraid

Turn Me

O turn me
in your hand,
I'll let you in.
I'll be the mettle
to cross thresholds
meant for trust. Feel
my new resolve, my
lunar cusp, each time
we shift our gaze
from what was us.

Answer to riddle in reverse: **yekesuoh**

Layers

I know her layers far better
than she. Scales that I peel
in a rush of steam. My tongue,
her arch, her bending knee.
The soft between her legs
where I redeem myself,
the way the Great Throwdini
did, who earned his life, her love,
by sparing them. Without her
bristling flesh, oh what am I?

Answer to riddle in reverse: rozar

My Face

You see my face
a thousand times a day.
I hunt you like a dream
in which you feel
the pull both toward me
and away
and cannot come to me—
although I wait—
as long as we are
locked inside this gaze.

Answer to riddle in reverse: hctawtsirw

Leave the Day

Then leave the day
and summon me
in the night. Your source
of light, my tongue
will show you what
you cannot see.
My rise and fall
will imitate your breath.
My darker side
will only be our rest.

Answer to riddle in reverse: eldnac

IV

Difficulties are things that show a person what they are.
—Epictetus

The Breakfast Piece

Milk crusting
in a cereal bowl.
Figs like little death's-

heads left, predictably,
untouched. A paper cup
berthed in its own spilt pool.

A still life
of the widespread type—
The Breakfast Piece—

that, in their rush
to school, the boys
lightly abandoned.

Remnants of a meal
or of a life? In all of our
formal studies, always

the latter. Pieces unexpectedly
arranged and surfacing
like orphans wanting care.

We move as if across
an oily canvas
to wash them, wash them.

A Drink of Water

A tactic for keeping us near, not for staying awake.
Still we'd call, Go to sleep!—quip that the well
was dry. We don't see our mistakes right away.
I sent his father pushing his whole self:

sleepwalker, his father's father, laggard
pilgrim. From across the hall, we heard a small boy drink
as if he meant to teach us how it's done: exaggerated
gulps, blessing of the throat, baptism. The sinking

thrill of water cooling his bony frame and head.
The playful gasp between each self-immersion.
The antics of the unconverted. Had he said

his prayers? His sadness at the question, his sour
objection. One more. One more dog-weary tour
and prayer was this encounter of his thirst with ours.

Synonym for Marriage

Pledge—bond, allegiance, alliance, a yearning
for a god; mercy, agape, grace; a chance against
the odds; a dervish dance; benevolence. In a
sentence: *The first love was cherubic eros, a child
with a flaming torch; gold and leaden arrows, one
to arouse—the other for unfathomable sorrow.*

Deception—duplicitous, the let-down, the Judas Kiss;
a double-crossing, ill offering; the trick among tricks
that colors history. In a sentence: *There was little doubt
in ancient days that Medea, slayer of offspring,
chariot-maid, was by a husband—by the stars,
by the forces of a spinning earth—betrayed.*

Forgiveness—pity, mercy, leniency. In a sentence:
*The Greek meaning for repentance is a stable
to clean,* its benches built for milking cows,
not a sinner's crawl; a purging of the stench
of an unkept stall; a never forgotten love,
Penelope's woven—and unwoven—shawl.

Faith—hope, truth, fealty, constancy; renewed belief.
In a sentence: *The Egyptians were sure that the vein
in the ring finger connected to the heart.* Hence, this
wedding band you gave to me—and which was once made
of leather, bone, ivory—has no ending, no mythic start
outside the beating of a servant's heart.

On Forgetting Ash Wednesday

Between the harvesting and sowing:
the stubble burn. Embers recycled

from a dying fire; the promising scent
of charred straw. Cinders inextinguishable

as newfound desire. The calendar plan
that out of the slag a new upright row

might spring: Lazarus flowers, roses
of Jericho. All this to call me home.

As if to dress me in a penitent's
sackcloth, when for decades—

even now—I would have come
on my knees: a girl in love with

high relief; stained-glass mysteries;
the lightness and the weight

of your hanging figure; the promise of one
love and end of days. Who else could have

sown, then seeded, this divide? Who else left
this shadowy thumb print between my eyes?

Balcony House

Mesa Verde

We huddle beneath a sandstone roof
afraid of dream-like depths. All around:
a cave metropolis. Two hundred homes
piled story upon story, rise to a mezzanine
of slick adobe tiles. Impregnable Balcony House.

Its builders crossed a narrow ledge, then threaded
a small entry that tests our king-size son
and draws us to the same high wall
the same sheer cliff that others slipped—
or leaped from—seven hundred feet, seven

centuries ago. They bartered goods, but had a taste
for gambling. As here, a charming reconstruction:
talus of tiny arrowheads, string of indigenous berries
draped, with surprising grace, by an open pit.
Exchanges we recognize: ritual gifts

for the chance of a woman's forgiveness—and not—
as our guide would have it—for the chance of crops.
Seasonal beads for an earlier season's omissions.
Shimmering talus, like the memory of a kiss. Plucked
berries for a city whose heights must have made them

light-headed, somehow unable to turn the earth back
to life. A stirring pool of cold, clear water is all
we hear today. Or perhaps, not water, but the buried
tones of chanting priests in kivas underground.
How could they not have heard the pools

receding? How did they miss the cracking clay
below? Perhaps it was our same habit of being:
an ever-promising season—men trotting up toe-holds
cut in stone to tend crops on a lush green mesa:
a vigilance they must have thought unrivalled,

while their babies swung from the ends of roof
poles below, to a rhythm sung from above—
quietly taking in the canyon's toll on love.

A Kenning

No room for a bird that sings
through her dangling foot.

Thus, always leaving
always grieving the loss

of middle-earth, things given birth
then quickly reified:

Something rising in a corner
swelling and lifting its cover—

not *bread* left to its own.
A swan's wake

more shimmering than her plumage—
not a *monk's glosses*.

A field burned for grazing—
not *poetry*.

The long goodbye, always counting
on some hollow ilex:

a kenning, a beggar, a toddler with one eye
and twelve hundred heads

up to his knees in water and lye
hopelessly lost—to take us across.

V

*Hang on to your youthful enthusiasms;
you'll be able to use them better when you're older.*
—Seneca

Invocation

In this bar's suspended lights, a halo hovers
over you. The tattoo that you stitched to your neck—

mythic spheres, a cluster of unnamed stars, a pyramid—
transforms to a sheet of muted notes, or a lusterless,

untraveled map once sketched for an epic plan
you had to separate, engage the three Fates,

their give and take, then bring your long tale
home. The bartender asks, *OK?* And though it

means a summoning, you nod and take another fill
from her tap; the glass like Waterford the way

you hold it still. It takes all you have
to drink from this new fountain.

To feel the sickening fall of cool, fresh water
against your stomach wall. To smell the souring

sediment of small bites of food. *Good boy,*
your mother must have crooned, *Open wide.*

And she must have mirror-opened her mouth too
as she spooned up solids pureed and fed them to

a vision, a mother's trust, a boy's long view.
Her mission, to nurture the god in you.

I am calling her here tonight—to your stool,
to this constellation of dying stars;

to this yearning—yours and ours—to this well
of life's water, grit and resolution, memories;

to the imprint of an infant I held close to me
still altering my posture and my scaffolding.

Calendar Plans

In the living room, a standoff—a deadlock
between right and wrong side of the law.

A boy bellies forward, holster and chaps,
motions invisible troops; his silver gun drawn,

waving in the morning sun as if to cut a map through
ranges unknown: cushions from a worn sofa, sheer cliffs

that fold, collapse, take their toll; his brother content
in a sheriff's badge removable for a change of roles.

How our memories tell us what we cannot know. How
in retrospect, days and months, our calendar plans

were a grace. How stars on straw costume cowboy hats
return like figures of forgotten clashes, traces of a

shimmering now: a new uniform, new boots, new hat,
new vows; occasion for the saints to be called by name.

St. Michael, patron of the airborne, stay with my boy
tonight, tomorrow, all the days. Know the two disparate

tones beneath a skein of geese—their flight so fixed,
resolved—when a mother prays, and when a mother calls.

Illuminator

for Geoffrey

In a light that you seem to trace
you see it now, its tangled shape:
a name poem like a nocturnal vine
started in school, but meant to flower—
to burst into bloom—at home.

Vowels already ablaze in carmine red
and verdigris. Glottal stops
that coil and link and knot
like tendrils finding their way
across a pleated page.

A manuscript of lists like canon tables
drawn in your own hand to answer
*Who is Geoffrey? G for gorgeous, great
athlete.* A fourth-grader's bravado, a pose
that I want to tell you

monks in your hunched position resisted
because they knew—alone in the listening night—
that the paint was theirs; theirs to make a pageant
of their own devotions, and not to bring new luster
to the daily rote of living.

And yet, your good apprenticeship
apparent in this trailing vine of watercolors,
apparent in this homely frame of references.
E, the wild look you see in your brother's face
and in the world: *Everything* girls want.

And how you beat us at our game
of self-display: lover of *Ostriches* and *Obelisks*.
Letters like ivied fences there to please.
Lists like crumbling columns of interior scenes
set into a folio of folding screens

that open—not to the ones who come to see
but to the screen maker who casts himself
along a linear leaf and works as servants do:
illuminator in his quiet cell; fold by fold,
changed by the paint as well.

The Bath

for an ill child

The slightest wrong move
could mean tidal waves.
Certain disaster
to a boy with everything resting
on delicate tissue—a bruised knee
to which you command a corps
of plastic ships—an austere (you admit)
but (you promise) heavenly beach
where men may lie down
in soft sand—a tiny fold
in your thigh—write letters
and find oranges to eat, plan
their next battle. Hard
that you know so much
(but you would shrug)
about these distances
from home. A trumpet blast!
You steam your mission out.
Predictably bad weather
and still another perilous gorge
of falls and fleshy islands.
The search resumes for citrus
or for some friendly harbor.
I wish you both
as well as a more
constant course—
and not another tour
of calculations
casually unchartered,
and not this
shadowy map
on water.

Sugaring

for Michael

A loyal maple lingers by your bed: nature fiercely altered.
Its sugar finds your pulse, then trickles in with a rhythm
partly boy, partly tree. For comity we call it *Mr. Pipes:*
a way of making peace with hard
adjustments. It takes long freezing nights and thawing
days to make the sap come like this—a big run.

Drip after drip, each steadier than the last, run
through clear lines. I see, now, nothing's altered
that hadn't already gone awry. Your limbs, thawing
in the afternoon sun. The only rhythm—
rations of sap met evenly, at last, with insulin. The hard
trek back from a seizure's arctic grip: whistling pipes,

banks of white cotton; a nurse (too cheerful) pipes
up: how brave you are, and you'll be up and run-
ning in no time. A promise? Or a wish for her hard—
luck kids? One spring, we got behind; buckets overflowed, altered
the ground below to a sticky mat that sounded the rhythm
of hard luck in thick, slow plops. The whole world thawing

like centuries of ice cracking beneath us, thawing
the gummy linings of blackened buckets and pipes
dripping with a precision suggestive of a subterranean rhythm.
I read, that spring, that scientists can tell if the sap has run
up from the roots or down the bark, but, not why its taste is altered
year to year. Always the questions we care about that are hard.

And "coming to" always the same: that hard
look sweeps over you. Your eyes, half-frozen pools still thawing:
late winter, but late in feeling the seasons altered.
Your way of banning ceremony, or welcome-horns, or pipes.
Your way of taking back the small reserves that run
from you each time you lose this fight. Your fitful rhythm

yielding to this old-world, pacing rhythm.
And knowing where to greet you, here or there, always so hard
to gauge. Which is the place of the senses? Where we out-run
our fears? You take us there, each thawing
day, it seems. Limbs or pipes?
We give up these distinctions. Nothing is altered

that wasn't already granted. Nothing is altered
that makes us see things hard
to see: the end of fear, and yet the whole world thawing.

VI

*Loss is nothing else but change,
and change is nature's delight.*
—Marcus Aurelius

Mandatum

A running bath, living water.
My sponge plunging,
then dousing your back
like a spoonbill, who lifts her large body
with slow downbeats and drafts.
Porter of waterfalls
to a drying marsh,
to the hushed flats.

Soles of your feet, place of encounter.
My hands a rush of white roses
that bloom and bloom.
Pedi lavium:
the flush of a body
giving itself over
to a prayer's
beating interior.

Your head bowed toward mine,
lectio divina.
You call me "Mummy" (our joke)
and with a halting,
trembling hand, smooth my hair:
a novitiate whispering over his beads,
or a lover who sees
himself cleansed for a leaving.

Learning the Scriptures

Molusco . . . Aqui . . . Aqui.
Bucket in hand, I follow

his lead. His silhouette
in the early light strikes

a perfect toe point—not ballet
but the liturgy's greeting

in a sun-steamed fandango.
The hard, muddy floor of low tide,

his stage. I see a clam spit
where he taps his toe. Plunging

my fingers into the cold,
black muck, I wriggle it out:

meal and sacrifice. A ritual-like
rhythm that the dance ignites.

When we steam the clams,
the smell of vinegar

and hops bubbling in the broth
overtakes us. A purifying incense.

Pabst Blue Ribbon for him and since
I am ten, Porto with *Ginger Ale.*

In the pot the clams flower and pop.
Pelican-like, he tips his head back to let

the fat belly slide down whole. *Delicioso.*
Body, blood, soul, divinity. Clean-shaven

for Mass. Brown. Azorean. *Vovô,* to me.
A welcome substitute to the homily: *Tap.*

Plunge. Smell. Dance. Taste. But not
in a faith, not in a language I knew yet.

Cues

I got rid of my landline when my mother died.

for Gina

Line in a fertile, buzzing ground; twine
like the curled, life-giving cord

whose length in a chamber of
membranes and underwater sounds

once matched mine from rump to crown.
Deliverer of sustenance; mythic shield maker;

fashioner of a perfect air; perfect
cosmos, perfect sphere. And from me to her:

wastes to be purged, calls for defenses
from a viscous, Delphian orb of still-blooming

limbs and senses. It is dots and dashes now.
A relapse or a renewal of where we started:

your profile in a passing car; a cashier who
recaptures your knowing glance; the chance

sound, in a crowd, of a woman's laugh—then your
signature sighing. Presences like parting joys.

Cues that the dirge is the wedding song—as perhaps
we'd known all along: the sudden breeze that catches

us off guard; the dog's inexplicable bark; the smell
of rain drying; stars at their brightest before expiring.

We Leave the Beaches for the Tourists, Mostly

and the history of tourism, a history
of our shadow selves: wing-prints of fallen
angels in shimmering sand, flapping,

flapping—the soul's earth-mapping or
a mating dance. Mouths, an upturned string
of shells opening to a vast and mythical sky.

These are the things they leave behind.

A paddleball court etched in the muddy flats,
where a ruddy turnstone makes his nest's
scrapes, space for a female's eggs; and

seagulls dive for nacho chips and funnel
cake and the sanderling's shrill song is the echo
of a mother's plea to her children out too deep.

These are the calls we hear in our sleep.

Or, the black-bellied plover's plaintive call
as he circles the shore for a sandworm
or a crab—or for something, something

to eat—and absently darts toward
a sandcastle made from plastic-cup molds
and a child's empty pail, pink or lime green

or gold. And a wave with a biblical thrust
catches them off guard: a torrent
of coconut oil and ocean spray, a sandal,

a drugstore romance—then the bright, shallow
meadows and plank. Kitsch in a tide's eternal
crawl and roll. Song and refrain.

Saudade

I used to take my friends through the back door
in order to avoid the ridicule.
What parents watch TV holding hands?
Or, God knew, maybe you were kissing her—
or more: taking to a Sears sofa
like lovers to the Ivory Coast.
Is it her frightened look that frightens you?
Come in the dark, then,
when she needs you most.

Each night she lies on the side that isn't charred.
A challenge in itself to face that way in bed
since it means not facing you.
A kind of Helen, but irradiated
and washed up. All this resting
on someone else's shore
like a miniature of the self
in stone. Is there a plan? Or, are you
suffering in some hell of your own?

Dolores, meaning *sadness,* in Portuguese. But you knew
how to brighten her. The "new kid" who could kiss,
you seemed delivered from a mythic place. And yet,
her girlish manner of brushing you away: hips leaning,
hands falling as if in an orbit of longing and withdrawing.
As if the two of you were swept up in your own play
or bartering—heart for heart, breath for breath.
How is this exchange any harder? Didn't you give
your word, and wasn't that blessed?

Of the two, you were the quieter one.
When you did speak, there was flourish:
You called her "Bubbaloo" and brought her cards.

You signed them "Leroy"—that face looking over a fence
that your war buddies knew. In every sense
her wants came first, her needs second
and us kids—a clear third. But, we were there
apparently to learn how
lovers love without words.

Labyrinth Walkers

They walk out-of-doors, hearts surrendered.
Quiet their minds to feel the spirit stir:
a kind of rhapsody or body prayer.
Not neighbors anymore, but labyrinth walkers.

Quiet their minds. To feel the spirit stir
some hum an Orphic song. To feel the leaving:
not neighbors anymore, but labyrinth walkers
neighborly in how they move and nod.

Some hum an Orphic song to feel the leaving
path become the path back in. Lovers of labyrinth:
neighborly in how they move and nod
like shades that have been with us all along.

Path, become the path back in. Lovers of labyrinth
become yourselves. Teach us your song
like shades that have been with us all along:
limping Eurydice, a glance never so tender.

Become yourselves. Teach us your song:
a kind of rhapsody or body prayer. Things lost,
returned in morning walks. Never so tender
they walk out-of-doors, hearts surrendered.

Song of Menalcas

Begin, Damoetas; then you, Menalcas, must follow.
You must sing alternately. The Muses love alternate verses.
                              —Virgil, *Eclogue III*

Damoetas: Sputtering stream from a garden trough.
            A breeze or a sigh. Green lizards hiding

Menalcas: among the Hawthorne brakes. A money cat
            casting about for cool and shade.

Damoetas: Marigolds tossed to a cedar deck,
            a plan to see them arranged.

Menalcas: Nothing else noticeably changed.
            O, who would have guessed

Damoetas: that this would be how to live
            alongside these dark jests: our daily work

Menalcas: and breath after breath,
            after breath.

VII

*Begin at once to live and count each separate day
as a separate life.*
—Seneca

Inventory

As in drill rehearsal for an embattled place,
we call in mirrored breadths an inventory, mime

in duet a list, a ruck sack check, that makes you gaze
at your wrist, check watch, check pockets, jingle car keys

chin-high like copper chimes, or like the bells
that focus our attention in the Mass, a summoning

that at the altar an ordained event—body as host,
wine that was blood—is happening and is past.

We are older now; this is what this is. A pause midstride
before leaving one another, before leaving the house;

a wave from the drive the way angels—disquieted—
watch, then catch us by the hair. They hear our doubts.

Leaving, returning, for them: *deliverance,* reunion with
the stars, a coming home. For us, *chance,* a constant drum.

Where Winter Spends the Summer

On a beach towel print of a bosomy mermaid
that reads *I ♥ Miami*. In an everglade's
wild plan marked with grilles and canopies.

Between concrete, leaning towers and a sea
meant for healing. In a daze, dreaming, gazing
at Odysseus' wine-dark deep. In the unclothed

body's prescient haze. On the front of a postcard—
a postcard painter's dream—in dabs of yellow
and green, intended, as postcard painters will,

to make a symphony of bathers between brush marks;
map out, in palm-tree fences, a new world: an answer to
the sirens' call, when all the bathers want is no world at all.

Sentinels

Love, you might wake today taking stock: birds
in their song, sweaters, socks. An aviary and a loom
that nature and two boys on an allowance keep
for days like this. A woman's palms that lift

toward your devotedness as petals rise and shiver
in rainwater. The bad investments: mail-order tool
set; a hammock (too short) languishing in the yard.
Intentions more than gifts. Avatars

that stay like sentinels against tired hearts,
photos tossed in a box; against rote recitations
of the Ordinary: our DIY-Credo, Sanctus,
Agnes Dei. Outside a thrush lingers, carrier

of wishes. What will it be? Another sweater? Usual
color? Or touch directing sight this early hour?

Portable Labyrinth

Moved by a quiet cyclone, a tarp set out to dry
on our neighbor's lawn lifts itself, gasps

and collapses, gasps and collapses.
You lightly suggest someone check: perhaps

someone's buried alive, or perhaps something's come
to mock our little dying acts. Eddies of light

drawn to a wayward canvas. Flecks of water
surrendering to a draft the way that love surrenders

after cruel words—breath by breath:
that mechanical grace that filters through the hands

and through the air when the self sees it has no choice
but to move toward a world of symbols and prayer.

In the desert tides of Reno, under the brooding sky of San Jacinto
men barefoot, women in patchwork cotton skirts

are laying down tarps like this—portable labyrinths—
on which they'll formalize our pilgrimage from bed to kiss

to river's edge. For a path, a cruciform quadrant
or a six-petal rose that calls up the Heart of Chartres.

And, for the blind walk, the on-axis straight approach
to the rose's core at the center of the mat: the mantra's

mantra. How good they are to make a prayer life
of the body's work. Or not goodness, but resolve, perhaps.

The same resolve that keeps us at our tasks: Saturdays
with our chores, Sundays in garden paths

lost in the rhythm of bowing and straightening up
assured our small cruelties are absolved from above.

Almanac

Winter

Love's humorless world
chilled parsing of promises
the heart's needs unfurled

Spring

Faith's growing season
promises seeded in lanes—
love's wet, furrowed plane

Summer

Dunes like bright altars
songs, epithalamiums,
promises, gawkers

Fall

Rank stems uprooted
good food, like promises, plucked
from love's good clay earth

Bad Apology

As in an endless rehearsal, I packed
and unpacked. The challenge,

you said, was to take no more
than I'd need. Tenderly, you followed

the track of a storm moving in from the east.
In bed, a wrinkled map across our laps;

you circled a town and highlighted a road.
A yellow, satiny, path. When we slept,

you tried the path, left markers
you had kept for days like these.

And the markers were keys. Clues
in a moonscape of dust-covered things—

a pair of gloves with suede tips; a scarf;
a ring. Ruins like proof of a marriage,

a story's skeletal sheen, small deaths, small
victories. Maestro, my mourning dove,

another chance? Put me back in that place
with its signals and gestures and promise

of more mistakes. And I'll show you
the hurtful lessons lovers make.

House on Fire

Too late to talk of causes. A faulty switch?
A pile of love letters left in an attic's heat?
Desire unveiled too late to relinquish

its sensual trail? All these, and love's capacity
to make a fearful pit, then send a Beatrice to us
in Limbo. O Mulciber, protector of the smiths,

sweet patron of civilization, of handicrafts; molder
of metal dreams. You conceived me, tutored
me; one of your handmaidens forged out of gold

and yellow flames. Beautiful corridor of fire,
transmuting ordinary days into shimmering reliefs.
I was the heat, the blast of stars rooting itself

in love's soft metal. I was the maker of alloys naturally weak.
Gifts that I hammered and hammered. I never ran from technique.

Arcadia

The city is sleeping in. Breaths
rise and part. Here at my desk

and on a kind of wing, I slip into a dream
that you seem to deliver: hips lifting

and rocking, heels digging in.
O, what kind of play is this?

Is it what is real and what is not?
What clarity it brings

about the mind's cool refusal
to over-script the heart's sense of time;

about the body's urge to live its life.
Pulled from one place, how naturally

it grafts itself onto another; how, even
in the driest season, we look for yield:

shocking pink blossoms from clay earth
or lilies from the dry cross-weave

in a chair of forgetfulness.
Or, about love's need to perform

what it knows—as in Rodin's
artful unfinishedness:

a passionate kiss, a woman's hips
turning on a mass

of roughhewn marble to which
lovers are always attached.

Interlude in Anglo-Saxon Lines

Waving and weaving
Through our wax myrtle

A swarm of swallowtails.
We hear new berries singe or pop

Before they flutter past us:
Palamedes, pipevine

And aimlessly, one painted lady, who
Pulls her larval purse from limb to limb.

This time, we take the tack
Of trumping them:

We stand here like two troughs
From Tripoli

Or, like Creeping Lantana
Languish here

And feel the fruit and sweetness
In our flesh, in the air.

Anthem

Portugal, 2018

No one makes love in European cities. Instead of sex,
a *café com leite* in a leaning café, bread and olives
like offerings or props between strangers. Between rooftops
blank bed sheets wave, flags without countries, on cable lines.
Hope for a better life ceased with the people's resistance.
In courtyards, dull statues of poets, cats in heat mime

a godless coupling. What lured us here? Films like *La Mime,*
or *Il Postino* where love is a wide-hipped woman's song, and sex
is an art: close-ups, pouting lips. College courses where olive
trees figure fertility. Lovers in rivers or on moon-soaked rooftops
prefigure holy union. We scanned tripping rhythms, limping lines,
foreign places, foreign minds. And your score-catching resistance

to hearing a true pulse in the troubadour's call—a resistance
that divided us then, steadies us now, in this sacred mime
called marriage. A bushman's song. In the flat next to ours, sex
solves a couple's dispute; breaths in small calls and answers: olive
branches; breaths in syllabics that drift over bedsheets and rooftops
like rhapsodies the ancients cried. Sighs that recall crossed lines.

Their post-coital calm, like a lingering thought, unfinished lines,
makes us pause. A halcyon: a sheer curtain takes air, a resistance
to differences in flats, in countries, in love's metered mime.
Bathing in light, we are fluent in all languages, fealty in sex.
From our window, an etch-a-sketch of intersecting lives; olive-
toned children run home. A round moon colors rooftops

beige-bone. In an alley, teenagers flirt: open vowels, staccato lines;
Whitman's free verse, Petrarch's cypress vine. A mournful mime.
For now, this is where god is, love. Desire's theater, wine, olives.

Afterword

*We suffer, not from the events in our lives,
but from our judgements about them.*
—Epictetus

As a young girl growing up in a shipyard town outside of Boston, I had little cause to read the ancient Greek and Roman philosophers of Stoicism. Perhaps our teachers thought that their young learners knew enough already about the subject. It wasn't until my tennis coach in high school gave me a difficult choice that I came to understand what the Stoics were saying—I could either stay on the court and play through my pain during a critical match, or I could sit down on the bench to nurse my injury. In that moment, I had an awakening that would come to guide my life forever.

I stood there remembering a story I had read in *Reader's Digest*. It was about flourishing in the face of adversity—and it was about Epictetus. The story related a time when Epictetus, a slave to a wealthy Roman master, was enduring a viscous beating from his master. When the tyrannical master began to twist the slave's leg to make him scream for mercy, Epictetus warned him, "You will break it." And in fact, when the master did break it, Epictetus simply responded with, "There, I told you. It is broken." Mind over master. Epictetus was crippled for life but went on to give the world a philosophy that for centuries has inspired and directed countless leaders, teachers, and students of life—to get back up when knocked down, to persevere, to favor the forces in life that transmit light, and, in my case, to not retire to the bench.

Stoicism—from the root phrase, *Stoa Poikile,* or painted porch—was birthed in an open market in Athens where the Stoics would meet and teach. This collection is inspired by that Stoic mind. A collective consciousness embraced by those that so loved the human spirit that they gave themselves to nurturing it. A chorus that calls to us not just to live, but to live well.

M. B. Fall, 2023

About the Author

M. B. McLatchey is a poet and writer living, writing, and teaching in Florida. Author of six books, including the award-winning *Beginner's Mind* (Penelope Niven Creative Nonfiction Award, Regal House Publishing, 2021) and *The Lame God* (2013 May Swenson Award, Utah State University Press), she is recipient of the American Poet Prize from *American Poetry Journal*, the 2012 Robert Frost Award, the Annie Finch Prize from *National Poetry Review*, and was a recent nominee for the *Pushcart* and *Best of the Net* awards for her poem "Smiling at the Executioner."

McLatchey is Professor of Humanities at Embry-Riddle Aeronautical University, Chancellor for the Florida State Poets Association, Poet Laureate of Florida's Volusia County, Arts Ambassador for Atlantic Center for the Arts, U.S. Ambassador to the HundrED global foundation, and poetry reader for the Miami based journal *SWWIM*. She received her graduate degree in Comparative Literature from Harvard University, Master of Arts in Teaching from Brown University, MFA in Poetry from Goddard College, and her B.A. from Williams College.

Visit her at:
www.mbmclatchey.com

www.ingramcontent.com/pod-product-compliance
Lightning Source LLC
Chambersburg PA
CBHW030908170426
43193CB00009BA/781

Praise for *The Mayor Has a Hammer*

Finally — a book that gets it. These poems capture the soul of local government with honesty, heart, and just the right amount of humor. If you've ever served your community — as an elected official or as staff — you'll feel seen, understood, and proud. And if you haven't, this collection offers a rare and moving window into what it's really like to do this work: the quiet frustrations, the small triumphs, and the deep commitment that keeps us coming back.

— Kate Colin, Mayor, City of San Rafael, California

It's rare in poetry to be privy to the minute particulars of a given profession. As the former city manager of one of the Bay Area's lovelier cities, though one not without its civic problems, Jim Schutz acts as our Virgil through the not-so-divine comedy of running a municipality. His tone can be biting, whimsical, impassioned, and/or funny, but his disposition is always one of deep concern for "the commons," and a profound appreciation of those who serve our local interests. As Jim says in his preface, these are really love poems to a work force too many take for granted. So, let him entertain you as he informs you. In these benighted times, maybe you'll find yourself among "Those optimists who inhale conflict/and exhale unity."

— Thomas Centolella, author of *Almost Human*

Who knew local government could be poetry? Jim Schutz did! This gem of a book makes you feel the joy, pain, and sheer craziness that come with being a public servant in these turbulent times.

— Kip Harkness, former Deputy City Manager, City of San Jose, California

More than ever in these times, we need those who honor words for their precision and beauty. Jim Schutz has done just that. He has explored the craft of poetry and brought it into City Hall, into the offices of government workers who don't get enough praise for their tireless work. We thank him for his world of "pensions, Ford Fusions, fluorescent lights, taxes, and gavels in the small chambers of democracy."

— Kathy Evans, author of *Trespassers Welcome* and *Imagination Comes to Breakfast*